Piano/Vocal/Guitar

glee

Music From The FOX Telev...

ISBN 978-1-4234-8725-8

HAL•LEONARD®
CORPORATION
7777 W. BLUEMOUND RD. P.O. BOX 13819 MILWAUKEE, WI 53213

Visit Hal Leonard Online at
www.halleonard.com

ALONE

Words and Music by BILLY STEINBERG
and TOM KELLY

* Recorded a half step lower.

How do I get ___ you a - lone? ___

How do I get ___ you a - lone? __

D.S. al Coda

CODA

Oh, ___ oh, oh. _____ 'Til now ___ I

al - ways got by ___ on my own, ___ I nev - er real - ly cared un - til I met you.

And now it chills me to the bone. How do I get___ you a - lone?___

___ How do I get___ you a - lone? ___

Guitar solo ad lib.

BUST YOUR WINDOWS

Words and Music by JAZMINE SULLIVAN,
SALAAM REMI and DEANDRE WAY

I bust the win-dows out your car
car.

and, no, it did-n't mend my
You know I did it 'cause I

HATE ON ME

Words and Music by JILL SCOTT,
ADAM BLACKSTONE and STEVEN McKIE

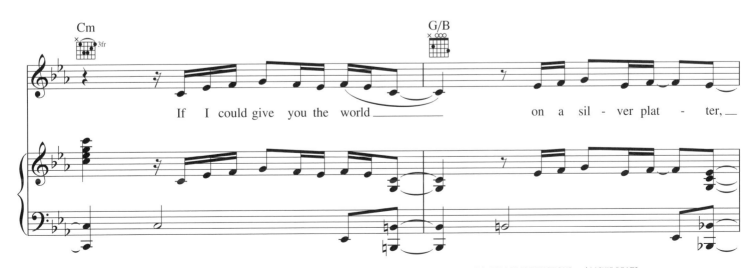

If I could give you the world _____ on a sil - ver plat - ter, ___

CONFESSIONS PART II

Words and Music by USHER RAYMOND,
JERMAINE DUPRI and BRYAN MICHAEL COX

templat - in', be a man and get it o - ver with, o - ver with. I'm rid - in' in my whip,

rac - in' to her place. Talk - in' to my - self, pre - par - in' to tell her to her face. She

op - ened up the door an did - n't want to come near____ me. I said,

"One sec - ond ba - by, please hear me." These are my con -

D.S. al Coda

fes - sions.   (Spoken:) This, by far is the hardest thing I think I've ever had to do.   To tell you, the woman I love

that I'm havin' a baby by a woman that I barely even know.

I hope you can accept the fact that I'm man enough to tell you this.

And hopefully you'll give me another chance.

DON'T STOP BELIEVIN'

Words and Music by STEVE PERRY,
NEAL SCHON and JONATHAN CAIN

Just a   small - town   girl, _____
Just a   cit - y   boy, _____

GOLD DIGGER

Words and Music by KANYE WEST,
RAY CHARLES and RENALD RICHARD

Moderately slow

She take my mon - ey when I'm in need. _____ Yeah, she's a

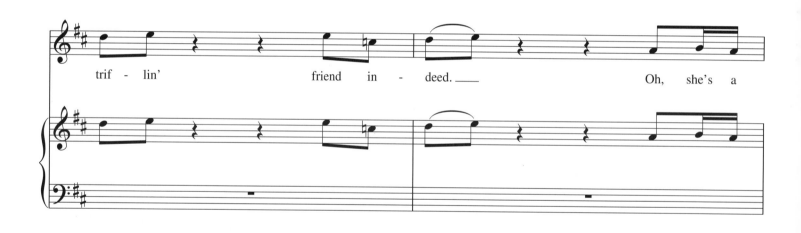

trif - lin' friend in - deed. _____ Oh, she's a

gold dig - ger way o - ver town, _____ that digs on

leave.) (Yeah, _ she give me mon–)
Get down, _ girl, go 'head. *Rap 3 (See Additional Lyrics)*

leave.)   (Yeah, _ she give me mon - ey.)
Get down, _ girl, go 'head.

Additional Lyrics

Rap 1   Cutie the bomb, met her at a beauty salon
With a baby Louis Vuitton under her underarm.
She said, "I can tell you ROC, I can tell by your charm.
Far as girls, you got a flock; I can tell by your charm and your arm."
But I'm looking for the one, have you seen her?
My psychic told me she, yeah, have a ass like Serena,
Trina, Jennifer Lopez, four kids and I
Gotta take all their bad ass to showbiz?

Okay, get your kids, but then they got their friends.
I pulled up in the Benz, they all got up in.
We all went to din, and then I had to pay.
If you fucking with this girl, then you better be payed.
You know why? It take too much to touch her.
From what I heard, she got a baby by Busta.
My best friend said she used to fuck with Usher.
I don't care what none of y'all say, I still love her.

Rap 2   Eighteen years, eighteen years.
She got one of your kids, got you for eighteen years.
I know somebody paying child support for one of his kids.
His baby mamma car and crib is bigger than his.
You will see him on TV any given Sunday,
Win the Superbowl and drive off in a Hyundai.
She was s'posed to buy your shorty TYCO with your money;
She went to the doctor, got lipo with your money.

She walking 'round looking like Michael with your money.
Should'a got that insured GEICO for your money
(Money). If you ain't no punk, holla
"We want prenup!" (We want prenup, yeah!)
It's something that you need to have,
'Cause when she leave yo ass, she gon' leave with half.
Eighteen years, eighteen years,
And on her eighteenth birthday he found out it wasn't his!?

Rap 3   Now I ain't sayin' you a gold digger; you got needs.
You don't want a dude to smoke, but he can't buy weed.
You go out to eat, he can't pay, y'all can't leave.
There's dishes in the back; he gotta roll up his sleeves,
But while y'all washin', watch him.
He gon' make it to a Benz out of that Datsun.
He got that ambition, baby, look at his eyes.
This week he moppin' floors, next week is the fries. So...

Rap 4   Stick by his side.
I know this dude's ballin', and yeah, that's nice.
And they gon' keep callin' and tryin', but you stay right girl.
And when you get on, he leave your ass for a white girl.

HALO

Words and Music by BEYONCÉ KNOWLES,
RYAN TEDDER and EVAN BOGART

Moderately

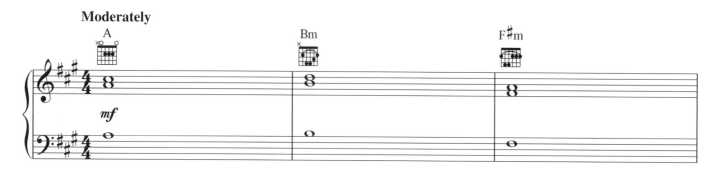

Re-mem-ber those walls I built?

* Verse one is written an octave higher than sung.

Lead vocal sung both times at written pitch.

Vocal ad lib.

D.S. al Coda
(take 2nd ending)

Ev - 'ry-where I'm look - in' now, __

CODA

IT'S MY LIFE

Words and Music by JON BON JOVI,
MARTIN SANDBERG and RICHIE SAMBORA

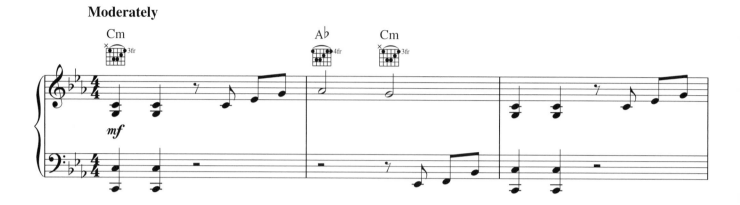

This ain't a song ___ for the bro-ken - heart - ed.
this is for the ones who stood their ground.

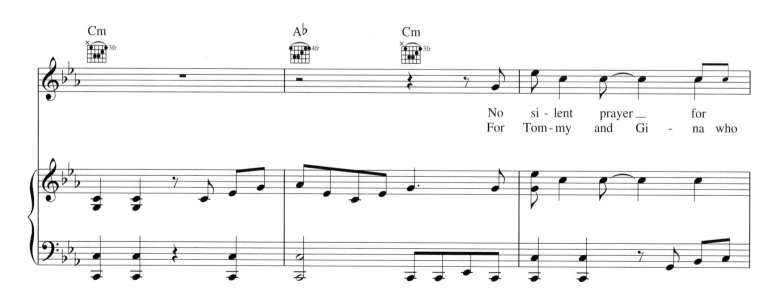

No si - lent prayer ___ for
For Tom-my and Gi - na who

KEEP HOLDING ON

Words and Music by AVRIL LAVIGNE
and LUKAS GOTTWALD

NO AIR

Words and Music by JAMES FAUNTLEROY II,
STEVEN RUSSELL, HARVEY MASON, JR.,
DAMON THOMAS and ERIK GRIGGS

Moderately

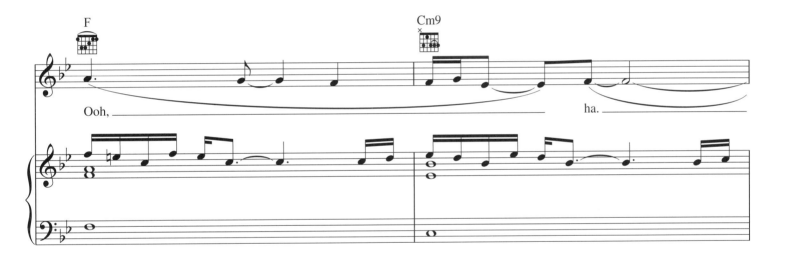

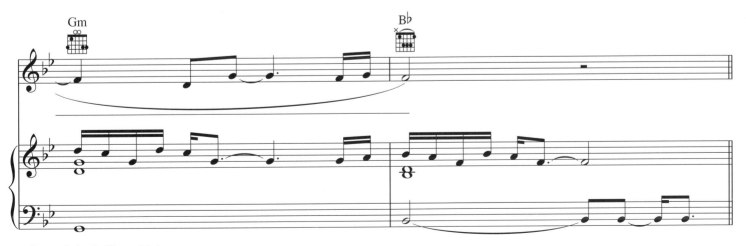

* *Recorded a half step higher.*

PUSH IT

Words and Music by RAY DAVIES
and HERBY AZOR

this dance ain't for everybody,   *only the sexy people.*   *So all you fly mothers,*

get on out there and dance.   *Dance, I said!"*   Rap 1 *(See rap lyrics)*

Ah,   push   it,   push   it   good.   Ah,   push   it,

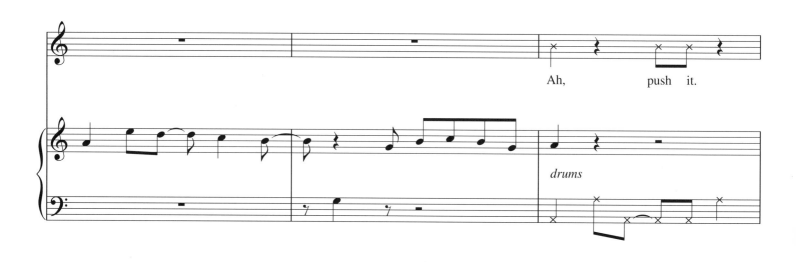

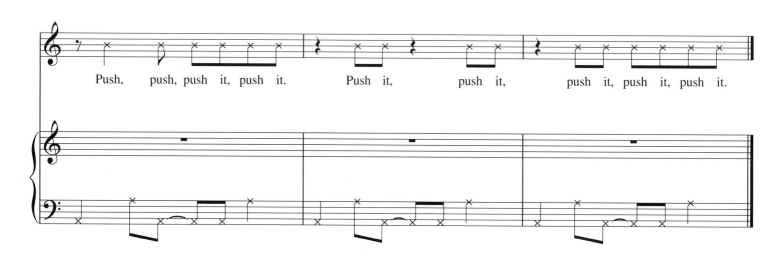

Rap Lyrics

Rap 1:
Salt and Pepa's here, and we're in effect
Want you to push it, babe
Cooling by day, then at night working up a sweat
C'mon girls, let's go show the guys that we know
How to become number one in a hot party show
Now push it

Rap 2:
Yo, yo, yo, yo, baby-pop
Yeah, you come here, give me a kiss
Better make it fast or else I'm gonna get pissed
Can't you hear the music's pumping hard like I wish you would?
Now push it

SOMEBODY TO LOVE

Words and Music by
FREDDIE MERCURY

Freely

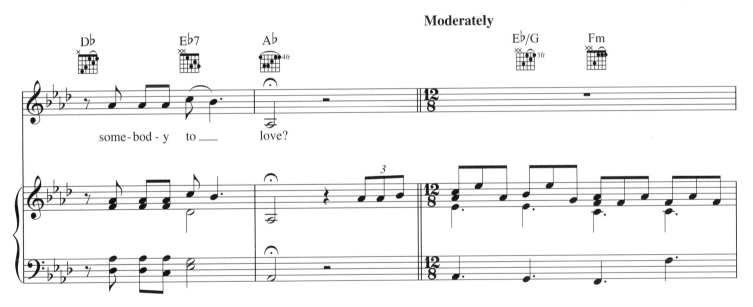

Can an-y-bod-y ___ find ___ me ___

some-bod-y to ___ love?

Moderately

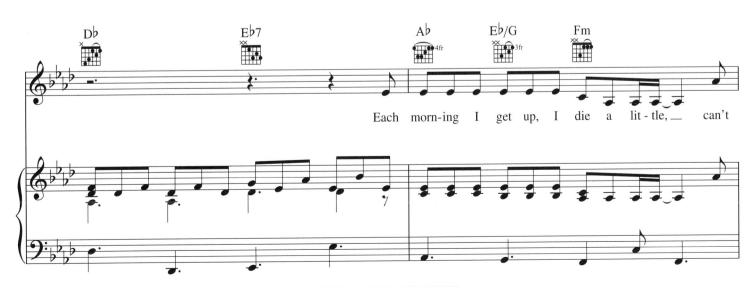

Each morn-ing I get up, I die a lit-tle, ___ can't

find me some-bod-y to love, ____ find me some-bod-y to love, ____

find me some-bod-y to love. ____

Find me some-bod-y to love, ____ find me some-bod-y to love, ____

Eb/Ab   Db/Ab   Ab

some-bod-y, some-bod-y, some-bod-y some-bod-y, some-bod-y. Find me some-bod-y, find me some

REHAB

Words and Music by
AMY WINEHOUSE

Retro Blues

They tried to make me go to re - hab, I ___ said, ___ "No, ___ no, ___ no." ___

Yes, ___ I been ___ black, but when ___ I come ___ back, you won't

know, ___ know, ___ know. ___ I ain't got the time, ___

and if my dad-dy ____ thinks ____ I'm fine, _____ he's

tried to make me go to re - hab, ___ I ____ won't _____ go, _____ go, _____ go. ___

I'd rath - er be _____ at home _____
The man said, "Why _____ you think _____
I won't ev - er _____ want to ___ drink _____

TAKE A BOW

Words and Music by SHAFFER SMITH,
TOR ERIK HERMANSEN and MIKKEL ERIKSEN

WALKING ON SUNSHINE

Words and Music by
KIMBERLEY REW

YOU KEEP ME HANGIN' ON

Words and Music by EDWARD HOLLAND,
LAMONT DOZIER and BRIAN HOLLAND

Set me free. Why don't ___ you, ba - by?

{ Get out my life.
Let me be. } Why don't ___

___ you, ba - by? 'Cause you don't ___ real - ly love ___ me, you just keep ___

Recorded a half step lower.